To Aoife—sorry for all the noise—with love always
JA

For Mum and Dad, who love to watch
the summer swifts arrive
CR

First US edition 2024
First published by Walker Books Ltd. (UK) 2024

Library of Congress Catalog Card Number pending
ISBN 978-1-5362-3148-9

24 25 26 27 28 29 CCP 10 9 8 7 6 5 4 3 2 1

Printed in Shenzhen, Guangdong, China

This book was typeset in Priori Sans OT.
The illustrations were done in mixed media.

Candlewick Press
99 Dover Street
Somerville, Massachusetts 02144

www.candlewick.com

# Super Swifts

## SMALL BIRDS WITH AMAZING POWERS

JUSTIN ANDERSON

illustrated by

### CLOVER ROBIN

CANDLEWICK PRESS

**T**his little bird, small enough to sit in the palm of your hand, is a swift. Swifts may be small and they may not be brightly colored, but they are the champions of the bird world.

Did you know they regularly fly faster, higher, and for longer than any other bird? Or that they may stay in the air for up to four years without ever landing?

Every year, common swifts travel all the way from Africa to northern Europe.

This is the story of their incredible journey . . .

Swifts get their name because they can fly so fast. Common swifts can reach speeds of up to 70 miles (113 kilometers) per hour. They've been shooting through the skies since the time when *T. rex* became extinct.

It's early April.

Mist rises over the tropical jungles of central Africa. Swifts are soaring high above the snaking brown of the Congo River.

For this female swift, it's the starting point of a long journey north to her nesting site in Europe.

The Congo is the world's second-largest rain forest, covering more than 770,000 square miles (2 million square kilometers). It's home to elephants, leopards, gorillas, and many other creatures.

Swifts gather here in the thousands, from all across southern Africa.
From here they'll divide into separate groups, some migrating to
Siberia and China and others heading north to Europe.

The swifts soon head west, following the setting sun.

   After a day or two of flying, our female swift is over the restless ocean.

Now and then, small green islands pass beneath her . . . but soon she is

beyond the sight of land, far out above the endless blue.

Swifts are fast travelers and can cover as much as 500 miles (800 kilometers) in a day. Their wings are long and curved, and their bodies are tapered so they can cut through the air. They have tiny feet, much smaller than those of other birds, and they tuck them flat against their bodies when they fly, which keeps them out of the way.

7

With nightfall, the swifts climb even higher, soaring above the clouds.

They are tired, but they will not land to rest.

Here, with only the moon and stars above her, our female swift closes her eyes and sleeps.

Swifts do not land, even to sleep. They fly up to 10,000 feet (3,000 meters) high, where scientists think they may take a short nap, allowing one side of their brain to sleep while the other half keeps them flying. Then they swap sides, so both halves of their brain get a chance to rest.

By the end of April, the swifts have reached the coast of West Africa. Here they will spend a few days feasting on flying insects, fattening up for their hardest challenge.

Before them are the rolling dunes and arid wastes of the Sahara, the world's largest desert. If our swift is to make it to her nesting site, she will have to cross this hostile land.

But she doesn't hesitate. She keeps flying north.

The Sahara Desert is both huge and very hot! The average daytime temperature is 104°F (40°C). Other migrating birds such as swallows and warblers stop off at desert pools called oases to rest and drink. But the swifts just keep going. With the help of tailwinds, the fastest can cross the 1,500 miles (2,400 kilometers) of desert in just two days.

How the swifts manage to find their way is a bit of a mystery. It may be that they can read the wind direction, or they may use landmarks they remember on the ground to guide them. Scientists have also discovered tiny magnetic particles in their beaks that may act as a compass!

By the beginning of May, the swifts have made it to Europe.

Thunderstorms rumble across the mountains of France,

but the swifts keep going through the lightning and pouring rain.

Swifts have to
keep clean as they fly.
They preen (comb and
straighten) their feathers
with their beaks and even
fly slowly through the rain
to take a refreshing shower.

After the long, hot days crossing the desert, our swift is thirsty. But she does not land, even to take a drink. She can catch the falling raindrops out of the sky!

A month after their journey started, the swifts have made it to their destination. The skies of Britain come alive with their excited voices. **KREEEEECH!** they cry as they shoot low overhead, screaming like fireworks,

**chasing,**

**diving,**

**darting.**

The summer skies seem full of joy as our swift joins the gathering, looking for her mate.

These noisy gatherings of swifts are known as screaming parties. Although we aren't sure exactly what's going on, this seems to be when unpaired birds choose a mate and older birds reunite with their existing mates. These exciting aerial displays are lots of fun to watch.

**And now, at last, she lands!**

It's been a whole year since her feet last touched down here.

Reunited with her partner,
our female swift returns to
a nesting box put out for them
on the side of a building.

Inside, they make a simple nest
out of hay, seeds, and feathers—
anything they can grab in the air.

Then they stick it all together with their spit, which sets hard like superglue.

# Our swift then lays three small white eggs.

Swifts mate for life. After a year apart, each pair meets up again in May at the exact same nest site they have used before. Tree holes, cliff ledges, and the eaves of buildings make perfect spots for a nest.
A group of nesting swifts is called a colony. Some colony sites have been in use for more than a hundred years.

New pairs of swifts that have to find a space at the colony are called bangers.
They fly around, bashing their wings on nest holes, "knocking on the door" to see if the spot is empty.

After twenty days, our swift's eggs finally hatch.

At first, the chicks are pink and naked, but soon small downy feathers appear. The chicks sit on the nest and preen one another, purring softly.

They grow quickly and need lots of food. They signal their hunger by opening their huge, gaping mouths.

OUR SWIFT DOESN'T FLY ALONE. SWIFT LOUSE FLIES LAY MAGGOTS IN THE SWIFTS' NESTS. THESE FORM PUPAE AND WHEN THE FLIES HATCH OUT, THEY CLIMB ON BOARD THE CHICKS. THEIR FLAT, TRIANGULAR BODIES HELP THEM NESTLE IN AND HOLD ON AS THE SWIFTS FLY. THE LOUSE WILL FEED ON THE SWIFT'S BLOOD, BUT THE BIRD DOESN'T SEEM TO NOTICE.

18

A swift chick may eat as many as forty meals a day.
Both parents bring food for their chicks. They catch flying
insects and spiders in the air and bring them back to the nest.

Swifts travel many miles to look for food for their chicks. Tired after her long trip, our female swift must be wary. Every time she flies out to feed, there is danger.

A hobby—a small falcon with vivid red legs—is fast enough to catch her if she slows down even a little. He attacks from behind, a swooping blur of feathers.

Like swifts, hobbies also migrate to Europe from southern Africa every spring.

A swift can catch more than 50,000 insects every day, packing them together with spit inside its mouth to make a dense ball called a bolus. Each bolus can contain as many as a thousand squashed insects.

Hitting full speed, she gives the hunter the slip.

That was close!

It's the end of July. Time for the swifts to return to Africa.

The chicks have grown fast. They do "push-ups" with their wings to get stronger.

Then, one day, they are ready. Ready to fly faster, higher, and for longer than almost any bird. They launch into the air, stretching their curved wings. Their sleek, dark bodies rocket over the rooftops.

Her work done, our female swift will fly back home to Africa—until next summer, when the super swifts will return again.

It's thought that fledgling swifts (young birds that have just left the nest) might even stay in the air for as long as four years! They will follow the migration to Europe each summer, and then, when they are old enough to raise their own chicks, they will finally land.

Swifts have been known to live for as long as twenty-one years. In that lifetime, they could have flown to the moon and back seven times!

THE HATCHED SWIFT LOUSE FLIES NOW CLING ON TO THE YOUNG SWIFTS. THEY ARE STOWAWAYS, ON BOARD FOR THE NEXT BIG JOURNEY.

# MORE ABOUT SWIFTS

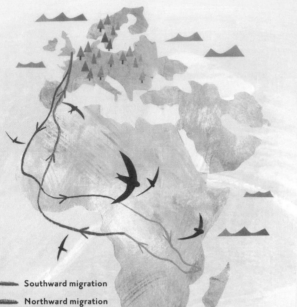

**OUR FEMALE SWIFT'S EPIC JOURNEY**

Southward migration
Northward migration
Winter range

There are about one hundred different species of swifts around the world; they all have some remarkable "superpowers."

→ **White-nest swiftlets** in Borneo nest far down in underground caves. Like bats, they use echolocation to find their way in the pitch dark. They make their nests out of their own spit, which, when stuck to cave walls, sets like concrete.

← **Alpine swifts** that breed high in the Himalayas and the Alps have been recorded flying at over 16,000 feet (5,000 meters).

← **Great dusky swifts** build their nests on ledges around Argentina's Iguazu Falls, the largest area of waterfalls in the world. They sometimes have to fly through the falling water to reach their nests.

→ **The white-throated needletail** of Asia is thought to be the fastest of all birds in level flight, possibly reaching speeds of 105 miles (170 kilometers) per hour.

The swift featured in this book is the common swift (*Apus apus*), which can weigh up to 1.8 ounces (50 grams) and has a wingspan of 19 inches (48 centimeters). There are thought to be 87,000 pairs that nest in the UK.

There are four types of swifts found in North America, and of these, the most common is the chimney swift. Like other swifts, they spend most of their life airborne and are known for roosting together in large numbers.

To follow the swifts' migration online, visit the Royal Society for the Protection of Birds' swift mapper at www.swiftmapper.org.uk.

## INDEX

Look up the pages to find out about all these swift things.
Don't forget to look at both kinds of words: **this kind** and this kind.